MINDFUL RUNNING

The best way to get happiness with meditative running

TABLE OF CONTENTS

INTRODUCTION

Running means far more to you than PR or a trophy for a finisher. It nourishes your spirit, lifts your mood and recharges your batteries. So, if there is no time, resources, encouragement or running ability, the effect is far-reaching.

Mindful Running is a feedback mechanism that increases awareness of your overall tension, so that you can avoid wasting unproductive training days, weeks or even months or that you cannot do something and make a save part of your life.

This training register will set your training background so that you can identify stress patterns and energy patterns that affect your running efficiency. You should change your preparation in an educated way to keep your running sustainable.

The effect is a better approach to training that helps you to get more out of and race. If your aim is to handle life stress, run a half marathon PR, lose 25 pounds or complete an ultramarathon, this feedback system will ensure that you get better and save your fitness, happiness and wellbeing all the time.

CHAPTER ONE
What Is Mindful Running?

Careful running is a vague word for many people, but it's just about being there, being a coach for consciousness and success. It's about mentally linked and not distracted within the movement. Distraction can take the form of other people, noise, technology, but societal influences can also come about. You know: How fast must I go? What is a runner's definition?

It is necessary to distinguish between consciousness and meditation. If we meditate, we take us away from daily life, from work, to pray in an atmosphere where we can teach the mind: how not to be distracted, how not to think, how not to be distracted from feelings of discomfort. Then, when we go out and run, we take and apply what we have learned during meditation.

Then you have to brush away these external distractions and stresses and listen to your body: what does your breath tell you about your body? How quickly do you want to go? The ASICS Sound Mind Sound Body team brings people together to various items, an appreciation and success coach. The breath is evident, some people link memories or parts of their bodies with previous accidents, and those associations open the door in yourself to more profound interconnections.

The goal is to get out of your conversation with society and return to a convoy with your body one after another, based on how much sleep you have had, how much you have eaten, how well eating was and where you are minded. The more you're attached to your race, the longer you can run.

How To Run Mindfully?

Staying engaged in an activity that appears to help you get out of the zone is much easier said than done. However, there are many ways we can train our body physiologically for Zen, and tricks that you can use to keep ongoing. Most notably, before the warm-up, the cool down. What now? What now? Think about it: 90% of people lead very busy, stressful and pressure lives. When you go to the gym on the way or from your office, you think about deadlines, meetings, your families. They are still in stressful condition, and then they will get even more stressful.

To take your body out of tension before you exercise, take a formal breathing position (return against the wall or lie on the ground) and concentrate on the air. One customer thinks of deep breathing into the lungs, which includes their diaphragms really. It doesn't need to be fancy, and it just has to slow down your breath, and you want to put it back to that slow breath every time your mind gets distracted. This is not the thing you can remedy for certain people in five breath cycles to calm out, and some of them will take ten minutes. Concentrate on your breath before you feel the difference. When you feel the relaxed feeling, your inner chemistry moves some gears down.

If you want to run attentively, you want to throw out some anchor points (your GPS watch, phone, music) that might annoy you. It doesn't have to be five minutes long enough to show you something.

Once these external distractions are gone, remain there concentrating on two crucial questions: How do I breathe and where am I looking? It's not about keeping a specific breathing pattern, but it's about decoding your breath to decide where you are. Too fast to breathe? Slow down. Try to breathe as best as you can through your nose. Mouth respiration is a stress response, so concentrating on nose respiration keeps you calm. And keep your gaze soft and wide, rather than centered, in your periphery.

You will begin to note the longer you visit, Puddicombe adds. You obviously get something about yourself, you notice more about your position, you notice more about your technique, learn more about your body, or we have learnt something wrong if we do not know.

How to preserve the benefits?

For your real cool down, you can use the same breathing exercise from your pre-workout cool down. You must clean your system out after a race, and you can't just stop from tension. The more your breath slows down, the more you get in touch with the parasympathetic nervous system that relaxes and heal.

Recovery does not begin until you are in a parasympathetic state. People miss the cool down all the time, so if you don't heal, you don't adjust, you just learn to suffer better.

Do not allow time (or lack) to deter you from this straightforward recovery phase. Of course, it will take 5 to 10 minutes after your workout to do some breathtaking work. But this is breathing. But breathing. You can keep up with your life and still use the very same resources at your desk, in your car, to get your body out of tension, and move on.

The better you do this during and during your race, the better you will be when you need it outside of the running.

Are You Conscious of Your Subconscious Mind?

You may have learned of the subconscious mind and how strong it is. Many trainers, speakers and authors who work in the area of personal growth related to theories and suppositions about the subconscious mind and how much our everyday lives are influenced. One common belief is that the subconscious mind accounts for 95% of our lives (some people suggest even 97%).

The most significant barriers to improvements in our conventional roles appear to lie in the unconscious mind, not in the tangible world of conscious intent.

Your autopilot starts up when you perform familiar activities such as bicycling or driving. So your unconscious mind executes the performance, that is, your acts. The same applies to all automated functions within your body. Blood is transmitted to all the veins in your body at any pulse without having to give the order. Stretching your arm may be a conscious decision, but the subconscious mind ensures that all muscles coordinate their actions. This is a positive thing, and it must work for you. You wouldn't even get out of bed if you had to think consciously about all the processes that take place in your body or how to do everything you do every day!

Your unconscious mind controls much of your thoughts and behavioral habits, even without being aware of the person in charge.

It's not your fault. Your subconscious mind seeks to protect you and keep you alive and does so on the basis of programs that are inherited or learned in your own lives.

In the first seven years, much of the learning took place. Your teachers in your world were your parents, family and friends, education, television, community and others. If you learn from an encounter that the world is a scary place and that fear remains with you, a feeling, something that you can see, hear or smell can cause it. You will feel it again, and your body will fly or fly, but you are in safety, and your conscious mind knows that you are not in danger. The subconscious mind will take over and run the stored software to safeguard you!

The subconscious mind is often programmed with convictions that have profound consequences for how you behave (or not act) in your everyday lives, which eventually affect what you attract. If you learned that it is impossible to earn money or that money makes people selfish, your belief system would penetrate it. This will affect everything you do and, by the way, your financial position. If you find that money is difficult and money makes people selfish, it is difficult or even impossible for you to gain and keep the money if you don't want to be greedy. Your reality represents your convictions.

Some reports say that we have some 1,000 ideas a day, while others say that we have up to 100,000 ideas. Most thoughts are repetitive, up to 90%, according to some sources, and many thoughts are negative and minimal. Most of the thoughts are unconscious and programmatic and therefore, are not understood. Neuroscience shows that recurring thoughts reinforce neural paths and promote the occurrence again of the same thinking or pattern. You're caught in a repeated thinking loop. The great news is that this can be changed and stamped. By learning to see these recurring thoughts and moving your thoughts and focus away from the thoughts that keep you trapped by practicing awareness, for example, you start creating new paths. When you no longer find yourself in the repeated negative thinking patterns, you can choose your thoughts freely. You take back your power, and you know whether to manifest.

A Beginner's Guide to Running

Running is among the most natural, advantageous and easy ways to train. It is relatively inexpensive, needs very little equipment from specialists and can be performed almost anywhere at any time. Calories are combed, the heart is strengthened, and the pulmonary ability is increased, though at risk for a chronic disease which includes high blood pressure, heart disease, and diabetes is decreased.

Running provides many advantages, but it can be difficult to make a smooth transition from inactivity to the daily pavement. This will show you how to go quickly, organized and slowly from a total beginner to a regular runner.

Step One - Preparation.

Previous preparation prevents the performance of the Royal Marines from being very bad! All this means that we have to make sure that we are ready to start our new routine and eliminate all potential barriers before we head off halfcocked. Let's discuss these important points to make the early stages of running as simple as possible:

* Running Shoes. For healthy and comfortable running the right footwear is essential. False shoes will make a nightmare fly! This is not that you have to hurry to purchase the priciest shoes you can afford. Costly does not always mean the best. You can certainly spend £100 ($200) on a couple of top-of-the-line shoes, but would they make you a better rider? Perhaps not! As a beginner driver, we don't need super light racing flats or high-speed shoes, and we need only decent coating and support shoes. When you purchase a pair of running shoes, consider using the socks you intend to run in and jog around the shop to ensure they feel okay, wear them at home for a day or two, so they will not cause any inconvenience to you and don't be afraid to take your unused shoes to the store if you are not correct. It should also be remembered that running shoes are supposed to last 4-6 months. After this time the coating begins to degrade, and the backing will decrease. Replace your running shoes sometimes to prevent damage to your limbs. When purchasing running shoes, make sure you get a knowledgeable salesperson's advice, but be mindful that they might well be on commission and that their recommendations might be affected.

* Clothing racing. All in which you are relaxed is fine to run, provided that you can freeze when you get hot or add layers when you're cold. Long sleeves and leggings may be helpful, as a hat and gloves could be for cold weather. A sun hat is necessary for the heat and shorts and a t-shirt might be better suited. If you are running at

night, investing in a high visibility top can help you avoid being a statistic for a road accident and light rain jacket for those damp days. Finally, make sure your running socks are snug and will not suit you with blisters.

* Running roads. It's worth getting an idea of where you can run before you leave your first training. Going on the roads is all right, but would you like to ride more in the countryside? Is your "home patch" really hilly and will make your early days more challenging than required as a runner? Is your path reasonably free of traffic, well lit at night, avoids any dangerous areas? We want to make your initial foray as simple as possible by minimizing as many potential threats as possible. Look for places to run in, not ones that make you afraid to start!

* Extras added. If you are those who like to buy other chances and ends to boost your practice experience, then it may be useful, but they are definitely not essential: a heart rate monitor to calculate how hard you are to work, a timer watch for your workouts (and the ordinary watch will be enough) and a GPS to measure your running distance, an MP3 player that will entertain you. There are a variety of other similar items on the market, many of which are considered to be essential but note, that some of the world's best riders come from the poorest countries and sometimes do not have to buy a decent runner!

Step 2 - Fixing a schedule.

The United Kingdom's HEA (Health and Exercise Advisory Board) recommends aerobic exercise 3 days a week, with a minimum length of 20 minutes, to improve aerobic fitness. It is proposed that these exercises should be done, if possible, on non-sequential days, for example. Monday, Monday and Friday.

It is a good idea to prepare where we are going to run before we even take our first run. Of course, we have to comply with the HEA minimum standards if we are to benefit from exercise. Look at your calendar and make 3 "running appointments" a week, so you know when the training is due. Treat them like every other appointment - just like a work colleague meeting. Do your utmost not to destroy them, and you will soon become a lifelong tradition.

Stop committing yourself in the early stages of your latest running effort – stick with the first three sessions of 20 minutes a week. This will make you less likely to miss a session, but even with the best in the world, the six 45-minute sessions you have scheduled will fall by the side, and your hopes of being a race will be over before they start. We can then add to it once we have developed a routine and are comfortable with it.

Step 3 – Let's go!

Twenty minutes of running could be an overwhelming prospect for an inexperienced runner who had laps of a football field while at training! That's why we will split our minimum session time of 20 minutes to run and walk. Our goal is to run more and less for the next few weeks until we hit a total of 20 minutes without walking. Once we can run in a single session for 20 minutes, the duration of our runs can improve, run faster or faster. We're going to cover progressions for a moment.

Warming up

We will spend a few minutes training our bodies for the exercise before we head out and prepare to hit the pavement. Oddly enough, the body will be going from a dead-end (sitting in a car or a desk or lying in bed for an extended period) to exercising so we need to make the transition from non-exercise to incremental exercise. This improves your running experience by making your first few minutes less painful, avoids injury and encourages your mind and body to get ready for exercise.

Since running is basically a full-body workout, warming up all the big joints, the elbows, knees and hips are worth spending a few minutes. One of the easiest ways to do this is by taking action at the foot of the escalator. You should feel a little warmer after some minutes, and your breathing and heart rate should be high. Next, we have to spread the lower body muscles, particularly the hamstrings, quadriceps and calf muscles. If you are not sure about what you want to do, check the internet or ask a fitness practitioner for advice. Place each muscle group in the lower body 10-20 seconds before heading out from the entrance. We're ready to go out of the door now.

Run/Walk

Our first several sessions will start walking instead of running. Walking is part of the warm-up and overall preparation, but also serves as a rest when we get tired of running. When walking, please make sure that your head is up, your shoulders are holding down and back, and your arms are relaxed, swinging freely. Drive your heels into the ground and push your toes away and walk quickly. You should feel slightly out of your breath and have to breathe from your mouth instead of the nose. This 'power walking' will provide many exercises with ample preparation in the early stages of our current fitness regime. If this is the case, keep walking for 20 minutes per session three days a week before you feel confident to try to run. I recommend you follow the same path for the first few sessions for 10 minutes from your start point, so you will have an idea of how much distance you can cover in the 20 minutes allocated.

If you feel good after a few minutes walk, I want you to break into a sprint. Concentrate on a heel/toe action, light feet fall and keep your upper body relaxed, and your breathing pattern is normal. Don't start a run, but you can keep it easy at least 1-2 minutes. After 1-2 minutes (depending more or less on your fitness level), slow down to your power travel. You can try to do your best to preserve the strong walking strategy we used only a few moments ago.

Repeat this cycle of walking/running/walking before you exercise for 20 minutes. Running and walking cycles are entirely intuitive, go or walk as long as you feel relaxed. If you feel tired, walk more and feel all right, run more. Remember that we're only beginning and have plenty of time to increase your pace and/or length.

If you've ended a 20-minute session (well done by the way!) find a gentle way to alleviate muscle soreness after exercise. After a new workout, slightly sore muscles are to be expected, at least in the early stages. Don't worry if, for one or two days after your workout, your muscles feel a little bit sore you haven't done anything wrong. It's just the body that says it's done a bit more work than normal.

Progression.

We now have a baseline to equate all subsequent sessions with the first instruction. The goal of the coming weeks or months is to go less and to run longer until we can run for 20 minutes without having to walk. You are in control of how the workout progresses. You can use a stopwatch, time your run/walk cycle, add a few seconds run, or use lamp posts as travel distance indicators just it's up to you. However, you plan to track your progress, and we need to consistently increase the time you spend and reduce the time you spend walking to our original target of running straight for 20 minutes. When you have 20 minutes to go without a walking break, stay at this level of practice for 1-2 weeks and get very used to doing that amount of training.

After consolidating our success and running consistently for 20 minutes, three days a week for 1-2 weeks, you should be able to press on to new fitness levels. There is a range of ways to make your workouts more demanding, and one or more of them can be used as you see fit.

* Option 1 – run more frequently. (Four days a week, for example)

* Option 2 - continue (e.g. for 25 minutes)
* Choice 3 - run more quickly (e.g. run to the same way just try to do it faster)

It is commonly recommended that we never increase the length of a single run or our total weekly miles by more than 10 percent at a time. If you run for 20 minutes, do not immediately raise your next run to 30 minutes, but to 22 minutes and so on. Increased kilometres/duration in jumps over 10 percent can lead to overuse damage. It is a better idea to limit running to 4-5 times a week and to ensure that 1-2 days are free from physical activity. The body is a beautiful thing, but it takes time to heal itself from daily exercise.

The first walk/run/walk program could take several weeks or even months to run for 20 minutes, but once you do, you will experience an incredible sensation of accomplishment and satisfaction.

And, once you have basic fitness, why not join a friendly running club or take a fun run? You may have high hopes to one day run a marathon or just keep fit, slim and safe. Regardless of what you want to do with your running, enjoy your running for a long time.

Using Mindfulness to Advance Your Running Experience

In recent years' thesis and study have overlapped in a fascinating and delightful way with professional practice.

After a time of research with attention in acceptance and undergoing counselling, I was able to adapt skills and material to teach and apply the skills to running experience, this book provides a resulting mental ability that you use when you run.

This form of the process is based on the classical body scanning approach that Jon Kabat-Zinn popularized recently. But I want to add that those looking closely at the subject would encounter some very similar processes in the field of gestalt therapy by Fritz Perls (1951) and van Vogt (1956) also wrote about a routine of body consciousness of the same type that was used by hypnotherapists in the 1950s.

The big difference, however, is that most iterations of this technique are written and done sitting or lying down, and you are always in contact with yourself. Here, if you are very involved and are moving, you are going to partake in the awareness process, but this is very different.

However, the main aim of this method is completely the same, regardless of where or how you do it. You just want to raise understanding of yourself. We do this by systematically increasing our knowledge of our physical sensations as we move.

I have also found practice in teaching clients or students, particularly if they nod or drift to sleep while relaxing in the early stages of their learning. The beauty of this phase is that you continue to be engaged in the inherent momentum of your running operation. You get a remarkable degree of absorption.

Evidence has shown that elite runners frequently follow an associative cognitive approach that keeps them in contact with how they work (Morgan & Pollock, 1977). It enables them to adapt and check their ability to push themselves further as they run or relieve on the basis of their knowledge of their body, strength and resources.

For this purpose, a process of understanding is advantageous. However, the advantages are much more than those obtained merely to increase efficiency. There is a great deal of evidence to support the benefits of our physical and mental wellbeing.

The runner has an excellent mental and physical health, which is promoted by focus, and such a practice often enriches and improves the pleasure of running.

A few quick notes before you proceed with it. Throughout your careful run, embrace the sounds, sights and sites that you meet and make the best of your ability to make it a part of your process. Just as you do, embrace your thoughts and emotions.

Do not try to push yourself perfectly to do this. Accept what happens all over the world. Don't always want to let go of those thoughts or emotions, just watch them, take an interest in your continuing experience, without intervening. That's significant.

Be careful as soon as you can. Enjoy the privilege of your time and be as conscious as you can, and watch it happen without any adjustments. If your consciousness is disturbed or goes away somewhere, then also acknowledge it, then put your consciousness back to the phase of awareness.

Only follow these steps to be aware of running, conscious meditation while running:

Step One: Start running and get going. Imagine that in this phase, you are smiling to yourself. If it gives you a soft smile, then it's ideal, otherwise, keep pretending that it's there.

If you run, start asking yourself what you see all around you instantly. Just give a personal statement on what you see, what you hear and the place where you run. Accept your world, enjoy it while you tell yourself what you notice. Grow and experience a sense of satisfaction for it.

Do it for a couple of minutes and then proceed to the next level.

Step Two: Now start shifting your awareness and commenting on your own body, emotions and sensations. Tell yourself how your arms and legs move, how you breathe, what sounds you make and note your own thoughts and feelings deeper.

Feel your muscles working, hear your breathing and experience running at this moment.

Accept all of your continuous interactions and grow a sense of self-acceptance and warmth towards you when you comment on your own situation. Note, when you notice your current experience, do nothing to stop anything from changing, just follow the path with the intention of running, do what you want to do with running and watch yourself.

Forget about the past, forget about the future, forget anything else and rest on your consciousness while you are going.

Do this for a couple of minutes and proceed to the next stage.

Step Three: Now, just spend some time breathing in while you're going.

Note the breathing sensations. Be mindful that your stomach and chest rise and expand when you inhale and remember how when you exhale. Know the speed you are breathing, see the air feeling in your nose and in your lungs, notice if it changes when the landscape changes as well.

Watch it, be intrigued and curious about your breathing. When you are running, your body knows how to take in the oxygen more than it wants, so be careful not to change it, look at it and embrace it, enjoy it and marvel at the plain pleasure of your own breath, feel it and adapt to it as you run. If you are distracted from it, embrace it too and put back your consciousness.

After you have done this for a few minutes, proceed to the next phase, if you do not want to continue for a longer time, then proceed whenever you want to. I just watched the breath and how it shifts over the course of several runs.

Step Four: Start moving your consciousness and spreading it in more detail across your body. With and part of the body to which you are transferring your consciousness, you sense blood flowing, listen and watch how you feel when you go and let it happen, embrace it as it is. Get aware of the skin around each part and the muscles working deeper, here are a few other things as you scan the body, concentrate on each region for at least some minutes, tune in to each area and be aware of each area in greater depth:

Start with your feet - see how they fall on the planet. Note their weight and strength as they influence the field. Note their weight while in the air. Sense the sensations as they move, note the bones and muscles and feel all the fibres.

Then step up and through your legs - note the lightness and weight that shift (or not) as you move. Note sensations inside each muscle, notice how certain muscles tend to affect others. Stir your consciousness into the knee joints, feel them move, and then up the thighs and hamstrings. Move your awareness deeply within, communicate with your muscles, feel them as they move.

Make your arms feel as you move. Note the angle of the elbows, see the weight as they move, and become more conscious of the muscles and the feeling.

When you respire, feel your chest and stomach - know how something shifts as you breathe, feel the heart-pounding in, see the lung extinguishing and inhaling. Note the muscles all over and inside as they shift.

Finally, switch your sensitivity to the head, neck and face. What emotions are you noticing? Know the scalp, the front, the ears, the voice, how do you keep your jaw, where your eyes point, where is the tongue in your mouth?

Notice all these things in-depth, spend a few minutes in each area, go into the details with your awareness, be absorbed into your area, and when you have finished the whole-body scan with profound focus, go on to the following phase.

Step 5: Now turn your mind and focus more fully to your own consciousness with this awareness of your physical body and the physiological experience of running. When you continue to breathe, you know what your mind is doing now.

What are your thoughts? Are you verbalizing in your mind your thoughts? Is your thoughts an emotional tone? Does your mind go through unspoken, nonverbal feelings, sounds or imagery? Be absorbed by your own continuous knowledge.

Then remember your emotions. Not only physical stimuli but also emotional sensations. Note your general mood and how you respond to that mood and react to your own ideas.

Note how your observations impact your thoughts as you walk. Note how your own running efforts impact your thinking and mood. Engage with everything totally, decide with great detail on your own experience.

Do it for a few minutes and then proceed to the next stage.

Step Six: Put as much as possible your awareness. When you feel your whole breath, your whole body, feelings and emotions, imagine stepping back and watching it all. So even if you were very well-tuned, imagine standing back and looking at yourself from a small distance.

See your entire experience from a very dissociated place, and you can connect yourself anytime, but do your best to have an interlude with this workout and to watch your entire experience running and being happily absorbed and committed to just being. Only be awake, nothing else.

As much as you can, maintain a built sense of calmness and peace as you go about it.

Do this for a while, then proceed to the next level.

Step Seven: You can choose to rejoin or swap each of the previous steps for the rest of your run. See if you can hold your awareness during the whole course.

If you are racing to a natural conclusion, or have to finish, interact with the surroundings and the environment, breathe deeply and spend your day a few times.

At some point after your race, indulge in some after-run meditation – after you have stopped running, think about it. How has it been? How did the feeling become conscious? How different was it from other runs? What did it look like? Accept it as it was and be mindful of the entire running experience.

Enjoy this, when it is done daily, it will bring absolute joy and your mind and body will thank you very much for this and your success.

CHAPTER TWO
Meditation for Running

As individual activities, running and meditation each have several scientific benefits. Running is wonderful for your cardiovascular health and less prone to age-related cognitive decline, and it also torches calories like nobody else. Meditation, on the other hand, helps to guide your mind towards increasing awareness and compassion for you and others, while reducing stress and anxiety.

No doubt, every practice can make a difference in your quality of life, but what happens if you combine running and meditation? Well, this is where the true magic occurs.

The connection between running and meditation

You could look at these activities and think: What could such a physically active exercise have a practice in common that focuses on mind strengthening? A lot more than you believe turns out. For starters, both practices rely on repeat measures to improve efficiency and benefit. Regardless of whether you strengthen your body or mind, repetition is the key to success. When done separately from your running routine, meditation will focus you more and will lead to better performance and bleed into your running training.

But here's the fun thing: why keep running and meditation apart when there's also a good and thoughtful way to combine them? Consider running meditation, bringing your body awareness while working in your fitness or training for your next big race. In conscious running, you focus on removing distractions and being connected mentally with your physical movement. Ultimately, it's all about your body tuning.

Five benefits of running meditation

No wonder the phenomenon of conscious running is on the rise. Meditation while running can enhance the strength of your mind and run. Here are some of the advantages that your meditation and practice can bring together:

• Reduced depression levels. In a study published in Translational Psychiatry, aerobic exercise and meditation were combined, and the recurrence of depressed patients decreased by 40%.

• Runs happier (and beyond). Davis found that meditation can contribute to lower levels of cortisol, the stress hormone, researchers at the University of California. Fewer stress and a general mood improvement lead to a run that is not so much about escaping problems as about savoring the nature and movements of your body.

• Higher tolerance to pain. According to a data analysis from the Wake Forest School of Medicine, a practice of consciousness can increase pain tolerance (the area of meditation that focuses on being present). If you relax and do not fix yourself on the point of pain, you can push it more easily.

• More energy. Restlessness and Tension can drain your energy buckets, but your body can rest and refresh its energy resources with careful running.

• Speed and endurance improvement. The direct result of the relaxation benefits that meditation can offer is an increase in running speed. When your body is comfortable, and without stress, it's not worn out unnecessarily, not to mention, your mind is also easy, allowing you to continue walking.

How to meditate while running
Ready to attempt meditation? Start by selecting whatever practice you are talking about at the moment.

Here are a few points of departure:
- Select a mantra. The mantra is a sounds repeated in meditation to assist concentration. There are endless possibilities, but powerful words and sentences like "I'm strong," "Stop running," or just "Right left" always are winners.
- Concentrate on your breath. When you run, use your respiratory pattern as an anchor and become conscious of its natural rhythm. You can also use your respiratory patterns and counts or try to match your breath to your foot strikes.

- Become conscious. Instead of allowing your mind to wander, concentrate on becoming aware of your sights, sounds and sensations. Is it a breeze? How does it feel? How does the whole body feel in movement? What are the sights you're going through during your training? Make a mental list of all you see and feel.
- Guided meditation. If you have difficulties diving into running meditation alone, consider a meditation practice for runners. Take the conjecture out of your first conscious run by doing a guided meditation.

Tips on How to Meditate While Running

Although most racers try to distract themselves by thinking, listening to their MP3 players or even talking on their Bluetooth telephone, the meditative course helps them to be present without distracting thoughts at the time of running. This is done by focusing on your breathing, the feeling of your body and its surroundings.

Why would anyone be more careful about how they feel when running puts tremendous stress on their bodies? Ask and reply. We must concentrate and remain calm as we push ourselves. Being conscious of our sensations moment by moment allows us to have more control over our bodies and to know our environment. This helps us to run better, in the right shape and avoid injuries.

Meditation teaches us to let go of concerns like tiredness too early and feeling pain. A meditative runner knows that pain and tiredness are a human being. This can help you to push through the pain, which is only a temporary state of discomfort most of the time.

So how do you meditate during the course of the day? Concentrate on breathing. Listen and get into a rhythm to your foot strikes. It can help begin a few minutes in a non-meditative state, then transition to a meditative state. If there is a distracting thought in mind, recognize it and return to meditation.

The brain is just like a muscle and the same way you bend and strengthen your muscle, and your mind can build endurance and tap into a 'reserve' that you might not even be aware of.

Here are Gardner's further advice and encouragement:
- Have fun. Have fun. Whatever activity, whether it's running, hiking or hopping, even if it's a challenge, it's always important to have fun.
- Allow your spirit to be free. There is little in life that allows you to feel free and boundless. That's what Running does for me. Find something that will enable you to feel that limitless potential.
- Feel and learn from deception. It's not always a question of winning. Short or bad day or race is part of the experience. Get ready to try again. Learn from mistakes.
- Don't be too serious about yourself. Even if you feel pressure from within or without to do better or be perfect, remember to do your best and enjoy the process.
- It's all right to be frightened. It may be frightening to reach your potential since often, there is an unknown element of how you achieve a specific goal. This can sometimes be a key driver for success.
- Find your mind training time. As sport all involve physical exercise, concentrating on your mind can give you a certain kind of perspective, focus and endurance that you did not know you could.

How to Run in a Meditative Trance

Running is a wonderful habit of gaining many advantages. In the beginning, and probably most evident, running is good for your wellbeing. It helps to lose weight and develop muscle, and it boosts stamina and overall physical ability. Running, though, is not entirely a physical endeavor; it also has a lot of mental and spiritual advantages on the surface. Here is how you can get the most out of your run by trying every time you pound the pavement to enter a meditative trance.

Next, you want to use running to help you concentrate and focus. Most people are at least a little ADD to our day. Can anyone really accuse us, after all? We are continuously bombarded all day long by ads, shouting media, e-mails, telephone calls and text messages. If we did not consciously cultivate and promote focus, most of us would live in a constant state of diversion.

During some job, you will improve your focus. Next, it is a good idea to just try to reflect on what you see and feel while running. Instead of emphasizing work or worrying about relationships, concentrate on the world around you. Remember what you are seeing and hearing around you. Pay attention to your feet's thud and breath speeds. Every time I reach the ground I like to hold my key chain and give it a sharp jingle, giving me a meditative sound that I can concentrate on every time when the mind goes back to life outside running.

When you can concentrate more on what is obvious and available to you when you are training, it's time to take the next step forward and start concentrating more on what your body does. Your breath is the best avenue for this kind of internal concentration. Pay real attention to your body and breath. Tune your breath's flow, rhythm, and breathing pattern and how it is synchronized with your body. Note the air coming and going and be careful how the body is moving with it in time. Be aware of how your arms and body move, how your legs are alternating and how your feet touch the ground.

Tuning the body completely is one of the easiest ways to meditate. It brings you totally here and removes all distractions except what most is pressing the rhythm and balance your body are doing and the world it is making. Being in a meditative state means being completely present, which means paying attention to this one of the most important things and then using this flow to release it. It helps to calm your body, mind, spirit and brings you in contact with the moment and all that is.

Tips on Meditating for a Healthy Mind and Body

Meditation was typically used for the spiritual development of the divine and the guiding influence of the saint, to become transparent and conscious. However, today meditation has become a powerful tool also for those who are not religious. In a world that is severely lacking in both, it can be a source of peace and peace.

It can be used to cure, purify and regulate emotions, increase focus, activate the imagination and find internal guidance.

When you start your meditation, set aside your standards and don't stress the "right" way of doing that. There are various forms of meditation, and there are no set criteria for correct meditation. What works for you is the best way. And figuring out what works could entail experiments and adaptations. I have mentioned a variety of approaches below.

However, when you start meditating, there are a few things to avoid:

• Don't bother pushing things to happen.

• Don't evaluate meditation too much

• Don't want to blank up your mind or follow feelings.

Nobody is "right" to meditate, remember. Only focus on the process and find the right path for YOU!

Choose a time and a place you won't be interrupted to start meditating. That itself could seem to be an unbeatable mission. There are people in your life who claim your time and energy unless you are a hermit. You would want to tell those people to help them find their socks, get their Get your gum out of your hair, listen to people at work, or something you had after a few minutes of peace and calm. Let them know that you have to do this for yourself, but they will also benefit, as you will be more relaxed, energized and loving.

You only need 10 or 15 minutes when you start your meditation. It's a lot of time when you get started, and it might well be that you believe you should pull yourself out of the busy schedule all the time. That's all right - it's much better to meditate for a few minutes than to put it off completely.

Over time, you may think that your meditation time is so useful that you want to spend more time in a meditative state. That's up to you entirely. A good aim is to work every day for up to two 20 minutes of meditation. Research has shown that meditation requires this amount of time to improve health and can help alleviate everyday stresses and strains.

The method is beneficial if you get used to meditating every day at about the same time. Some people find that meditation works for them first in the morning. Others meditate last night before they go to sleep. There is no precise time for anyone. Anything that works for you is fine! Only make sure you practice daily.

The place you choose to meditate is up to you again. Some people put a room aside in their meditation room in their home, but if you start out, it is probably a little too serious. Instead, in your bedroom, the lounge, the kitchen or even the garden – anywhere you feel least troubled. It's best if you don't try meditating in the living room while the rest of your family watches TV, of course. Besides that, it does not matter the exact place where you meditate - it is much more important than you begin to meditate.

If you think you don't fit for the original position you picked, don't be afraid to change it. The same applies to the time and method you have chosen. The overall value of meditation goes way beyond the exact meditation technique that you use to gain an advantage.

Guided meditation is the easiest ways to start meditation. This is a CD or MP3 with all the guidance for achieving a meditation status. You only need to find out where you're not going to be disturbed, sit or lie down and play the audio file. Soundstrue.com has many guided images and music for meditation.

Many kinds of meditation exist. We will cover the popular styles, but if none of these suits you, there will be many more on the Internet to explore. Feel free to play with any of the following different meditations before you find a meditation which works well for you.

Centering

This is meditation action. There is a place within you which is always calm and peaceful. This place is often called your "calm center" Centering means remaining in your peaceful center in the middle of daily life. Centering implies that your inner light is not overshadowed by stressful conditions or negative feelings and behaviors.

If you focus, you are in a state of clarity, concentration, peace and balance. You are unclear, unfocused, stressed and unbalanced when you are not focused.

An excellent centering technique requires little attention and will allow you to take care of the activity, such as washing plates, folding laundry, or gardening. Be aware, however, that if you see something, your family is more tempted to interrupt. Just tell them that you are also meditating and that they should leave you alone for a few minutes if they do not want to help you do dishes, laundry facilities or garden. Here are a few fast centering techniques.

Simple Awareness of Breath

During your involvement in anything you do, focus on your breathing for a few moments. It doesn't have to be your complete attention only enough to return you to your core of calmness. Breathe normally, or maybe a little slowly and profoundly.

Your energy recovery

If you feel overwhelmed and dispersed, take a few long, slow breaths. Imagine with every inhalation, all of your distributed energy and focus is drawn back to your inner self and your source of peace.

Let's go

It's advantageous when you're tense and/or fixated on tension or negative thought or emotion. This centering strategy blends breath awareness with a word or mantra, "Let go." Say (silently or aloud) "Let" as you inhale. Tell "go" as you exhale... while you let go of all that stresses you.

Relaxation Meditation

This surprisingly comfortable and restful meditation uses a little-known eye secret. Allowing the eyes to relax in a soft descending gaze has a relaxing effect instantaneously.

Relaxation meditation offers a lot of stress relief and can be used almost anywhere for a fast two-minute relaxation break (but not while driving). You may also realize an increased perception.

Sit securely straight with your spine.

Enable your eyes to rest comfortably down, look softly, but concentrate on nothing.

Enable your eyelids to fall to a level that feels most relaxed without fully closing your eyes.

Continue to look down, and the gaze is your primary subject (rather than the area at which you are gazing). You will note more rhythmic breathing.

It's all right to let your attention wander a little. If your eyes get really heavy, letting them close is OK.

If you miss your relaxation, just put your focus back to your relaxed downward look.

Breathing Meditation

You will concentrate on your breath in this meditation. This is possibly one of the best meditation techniques, to begin with.

Begin by taking a comfortable spot. When you sit meditating, sit comfortably and straight with your spine. This encourages the divine energy to freely flow up the backbone, an essential part of meditation. Leaning against the back of the chair, a wall, a headboard etc. is okay. If you can't sit up for physical reasons, lie flat on your back. Place your hands in any comfortable position.

Close your eyes until you're relaxed.

Begin to feel your breath. We respire so much that we take breathing as a matter of routine. Take the time to see your breath.

Note the air your lungs are filling.

Then remember that you breathe out and your lungs leave the air. Repeat the method of breathing note.

You will notice ideas coming up when you do this. They may be about family, friends, work or something else. It doesn't matter - it's all part of the process, and it's very natural to keep thinking during your meditation.

But if these thoughts come up, let them with your next breath float away. Take your mind back to concentrate on your breathing any time your thoughts wander.

Meditation on Walking

If it is hard to sit still and keep your eyes closed while meditating, walking meditation might be good for you.

Walking meditation has four components:

- Be mindful of your respiration
- Note the atmosphere
- Be aware and attentive to the movement of your body
- Take time to reflect on your experience of meditation

Be mindful of your breathing as you would in the course of breathing meditation. Note every breath and then breathe out again.

Be mindful of the air that fills your lungs and use every exhalation to send intrusive thoughts.

If you begin to notice your world, you will probably be amazed. In our daily lives, we take a lot of things for granted, and half of what is around us is totally unnoticed. When you walk outside, note the various colors you see.

Don't note colors only. Notice colors. Listen for sounds. Listen for sounds. There might be bird songs, road traffic, and people or animals talking. Tune into these various sounds consciously. Note the many songs the birds sang.

Pay attention to the various traffic sounds while you are in an urban environment. The engine of each car sounds different slightly. So does the wheels sound on the multiple surfaces of the roadway? You will find yourself listening to stuff that only existed before you.

You can also fill the senses with smells. Perhaps the scent of freshly mown grass or the sweet smell that happens right after a rain shower. There are plenty of smells in the world, and most of them certainly have passed your consciousness.

Begin to feel the light pressure on your feet's soils when you walk. You know the air that touches your skin, whether it's a calm day or a windy day. Pay attention to the rotation of your body as you walk. Feel like your arms are swinging. Note how you keep your head - is it straight and careful, or an alternate position? Take care of various parts of your body as you walk, and you will be intrigued by what you see.

After your walking meditation is over, take a little time to return to your normal life. During this time, go by your feelings and thoughts during your meditation period mentally. Think about what you can do to further improve your experience when you plan to do a walking meditation.

Gradually, return to your normal world from your peaceful site.

Meditation of Universal Mantra

This meditation is based on an ancient Indian text called Malini Vijaya Tantra, which dates from approximately 5000 years ago. It is effortless and yet effective meditation in its ability to relax your mind and bind you to your essence or Inner Spirit.

This meditation uses a mantra as your focal point. A mantra can catalyze a change to a deeper and more peaceful consciousness. The mantra most widely used in this meditation is Aum. Aum has no literal translation. Instead, it is the universe's fundamental vibration. If you were to tap into the real sound of the universe, you would note the eternal sound of Aum.

While this mantra is often sung aloud, you can repeat the mantra in this meditation mentally. Silently.

Before we hit the actual steps, we need to be conscious of a few essential points:

- Meditation keys are to repeat the mantra in your mind slowly or softly.
- The strength of this technique is that you let go and allow your attention to fall into the depths of consciousness.
- So while you concentrate on the mantra, it is not the purpose of this meditation to remain focused on the mantra.

- Trying to remain centered would prevent you from going down to the deeper realms. You will instead repeat the mantra of "minimal effort" and allow your mind some room to wander.
- Resist the temptation of doing something and let the mantra do the job.

This meditation quickly results in a change to deeper, happier states of consciousness. (The degree of this varies from one session to another) It increases the flow of energy through the brain and eliminates a lot of physical and emotional toxins.

This detoxification means that it is best to hold this meditation at first, starting ten or fifteen minutes a day. After a month or so, it could be increased to twenty minutes, but for those without many years' experience in meditation, this should be limit. It is suitable to drink plenty of water.

Eventually, mantra meditation speeds up spiritual development as you enter a state of calm and awareness of yourself.

Sit comfortably, with closed eyes and a relatively straight back.

Start to gently repeat the mantra in your head.

Repeat the mantra at the most normal tempo. No need to synchronize the mantra with your breathing, but it's all right if that happens naturally.

Enable the mantra to appear in your mind more faintly. Repeat it with little effort.

Continue to tenderly repeat the refrain and encourage something to happen.

If you find you fall into a sleepy or dreamlike state at any time, allow it to happen.

If and when you know that your mind has moved totally away from the mantra, start repeating it again and continue with little effort.

Stop repeating the mantra after 10 or 15 minutes and slowly come out of your meditation.

Give yourself a time to enjoy the sensation of floating and relaxation around you after some technique of meditation. Take a deep breath, gird your loins and wander into your everyday life with fresh vitality and a deep sense of calm.

The Science of Mind

The science of mind has been extended to the experiments that exploit the state of mind at various stages of consciousness. Brain research as connections to the different behaviors and features of brain waves led to the advancement of the mind science. Today, the advantages obtained by inducing brain waves to reach those frequencies by technology can be accomplished, and the body is accompanied by the reaction. The science of the mind should lead to solutions concerning the mind and state of it, rather than to solutions such as drugs and dependency. The latter can lead to additional complications.

There are no limitations to the technology. It has contributed to millions of issues and difficulties being minimized and removed. It is applied in culture, even when users had no knowledge about its use, in areas such as music. You will find that you won't need solutions like medications to help you sleep or relax with technology. These alternatives are costly and cause side effects and addiction to your health to be detrimental. The subconscious can be attained through the solution of music to release previously in mind negative thoughts and mental experiences.

The elimination of negative impressions and the release of negative feelings will achieve greater liberation from previously achieved conditions. After complete recovery, the individual can attain a true spiritual incarnation. You will undergo a remarkable spiritual transformation through access to the states of consciousness. Knowing how to handle your whole dimension is vital for your overall health. The technology of brainwave training will help to clean the subconscious thoroughly for a spiritual transition.

Mental science has created the manipulation of so-called induced states of consciousness. This is known as brainwave training, which synchronizes the brainwaves with physical frequencies for desired results such as relaxation, sleep, concentration, decreased stress and more. The positive thing about brainwave training technology is that it is cost-effective and inexpensive and can be applied at home without the help of a professional when experienced.

You must be prepared with information about the influence of profound meditation on the human psyche because the results are incredible. While it is many times new and confused to apply this knowledge to Western cultures and esoteric practices, it is known to the eastern and western esoteric traditions. The research focuses on the ability of different monks and experienced eastern meditators to achieve different improvements in brainwave patterns.

Studies have explained the mind and the metaphysical ramifications of meditation, but it has only been the entire surface. If you want to purify your mind from past conditioning, you must go through deep meditation. And this is the only solution for your knowledge. Real spiritual awakening can result from deep meditation, but it can only be achieved by reprogramming the mind (neuro-linguistic programming (NLP)). Positive reinforcement is often implemented for the same purpose but does not create solutions close to profound meditation.

CHAPTER THREE

Mindfulness Exercises

Habits rule people's lives. The quality of life will rely on the habits that you have chosen to create. When the time that is spent in subconscious reaction instead of in genuine action is understood, one will want to accept the practice of consciousness.

Mindfulness activities are the rational road to establishing a system of conscious and dedicated living. Mental distraction is the condition to some extent for most people. Therefore so many people are able to perform several tasks. Multi-tasking can be a source of pride for others, as a true machine.

Practice activities can help to cultivate the habit of remembering the humanity of our existence. For many people, modern life prevents monastic life. Monastic life is an excellent platform for discovering one's spiritual existence.

However, conscientiousness lessons in daily chaos offer an incredible opportunity for hands-on living. The gentle and persistent effort to remember one's true nature in the mess of modern life is the practice which can gradually improve the link with the divine.

Ideally, your determination to set aside time for calm meditation every day will be an excellent course of action. This could be unlikely, in fact.

The age-old method of monitoring the breath is a consciousness practise that can function for anyone. The beauty of this easy exercise is that we're never breathless. We cannot ignore breathing in the most difficult situations. In the middle of any operation, we should still be attentive to the breath, and this basic technique allows us to remind ourselves.

As irrelevant as it may sound, the person who is able to master the simple technique in the hectic modern everyday routine may have achieved more through the growth of consciousness than the guru isolated in a convent.

The practice of thoughtfulness is not meant to establish a grandeur of sublimity as much as it is a prosaic reminder of the marvel of life. It's not for the few selected but rather the essence of all, and I can tell all.

Any time circumstances cause distress and disconnection, just take a moment to remember the breath. Slow and gentle inhalation or exhalation will alert you instantly that you are alive human. Regardless of the physical situation, you're in a more independent mental situation. The way you recall your breath will allow careful approaches to the demands of life.

The ability to act rather than respond is not a reactive but engaged person.

Mind Exercises for Success

Mind exercises are helpful in developing the natural creative powers with which we were born. Some people find visualization and mental manipulation difficult to do as they get older. Since creativity age and stress override optimism, it is difficult to take the time to improve those mental abilities. It is only as children that we naturally play the freedom of imagination in our environment, and it is unfortunate. And to master your mind, your life is to be mastered, and the following exercises of mind will help you.

Alter Your Habitat

The first of these powerful mental exercises I want to share with you focuses on your environment. You can do it anywhere and everywhere. A man named John began using this mental tool in the local gym. During his workouts, he realized that the more people that appeared, the more irritated he became. He knew this was no concern for anyone but his own. In the early hours of the morning, he only needed extra privacy. Instead of feeling irritated, he decided to change his mood and start my day with an excellent positive mindset without changing his routine.

He did this by imagining how the fitness center would look if he were alone there, right now! Then he cleaned out all the distractions around him piece by piece. He concentrated his attention only on the sounds he heard and empty exercise machines AS IF no one but himself were present. With a little practice that really studied this method, he could feel as comfortable at all times of the day in the gym, regardless of the number of people present as though he were all alone!

Another example is a hot summer day. It is easy to focus on the causes of our discomfort when we are stressed. Try to concentrate on the opposite, regardless of how far away from reality, for a refreshing change! Your mind regulates all of your body's biomechanical activity. Imagine the feel of the cold temperatures below zero in the middle of winter, the next time you take a 90-degree stroll. This technique can be used in innumerable ways, and the more efficient it is for you. Your creativity is the answer, but what really makes it work is to make it work! This allows you to feel the feelings connected to the sensations in your brain about the mental pictures on which you concentrate. This is precisely the same way we attract anything into our lives!

Feel from Afar

Like many mental exercises, this one is both fun and challenging. It is very fundamental in concept but takes patience to build real skills. When it comes to imaginative visualization and attraction, people who excel in making this technique their main mind exercises still seem to have an edge!

Begin with something common like a warm cheeseburger. Feel it and try to note that it's the same feeling, the scent, and the look. Concentrate on the details such as the bun texture and the condiments smell on it. Now just move away and go to another room. Try to feel the Same sensations that you have had before, except at this moment without actually holding the cheeseburger! Take a while to relive the experience. Feel the warmth and texture, smell it as well as you can recall, see it in all details. Do so until you can't believe it's not in your hands!

Mind exercises such as this prepare the minds to build something you can imagine. This strengthens the strength and efficiency of any goal you try or feel you want to attract. Try to feel random things from afar with your mind, from your sofa in the building to the fruit in the supermarket. Just pick something and concentrate all your senses until you don't even have to be close to it!

Overcome All

My favorite of all good mind exercises is the constructive attraction principle. It is a method of self-esteem adjusted to improve creative capacity. You just need to believe in one thing to make things work for yourself. As long as you are on your side, this tool allows you to break any boundary or "mental attack" anyone can break out. It's fighting 101, and if more people were using this technique, the world would be a lot better!

In principle, you need to understand that if you allow it, the only way anyone can harm you mentally and emotionally. You need your consent. Since you can only be hurt by a statement, look or behave outside, if you believe that you're the person they try to show you that they think you are! Often this person doesn't really believe that himself, he only wants to hurt you by making you feel like that because that is how he feels inside. That's why your family and friends will hurt you the most. You believe them faster than a stranger instinctively, even more than yourself.

Now that we know that you have to agree with the negative feedback to send out the negativity, you have the information to use this tip. Stop it! Stop it! Choose to DISAGREE with any negative thinking, emotion, or mental picture that comes into your mind. Do not respond automatically with the self-defense anger mechanism or let yourself be victimized as if you are guilty. To send out such a negative response, you just get more negative feedback. Thus, the more you let those dark emotions go, the more intense the negativity returns! The WORST you can do to yourself is to agree and give back what the person has sent you. If you want to support yourself, spread it in your mind. Know and say that you don't agree with the person in your mind. You have no excuse to be angry or hurt. You don't have to answer with anything other than compassion because in your opinion you are worth it. You're intelligent, healthy, beautiful, and you don't agree with someone who wants to make you feel different. Forgive them and in exchange, offer compassion. A silent compliment to their highest quality, or if you can simply don't worry about them, your will ensures more positive outcomes in your life. Protect yourself and others by seeing the BEST of you, as you are worth protecting.

Possibly the toughest of the mental exercises I know. It's not what comes naturally to forgive those who hurt us. It needs real strength and high self-esteem. Train and adhere to it. People who want to hurt you are trying to make you feel bad instinctively. That's because they know your day and even your life will be ruined. Bad effects contribute to negative effects in your life. Positivity leads to positiveness in your life. Take charge of the circumstances by refusing to make others feel bad. Instead, bless them with a good thought and raise your profit ten times. You can either accept your kindness and improve yourself or make your negative thinking worse and curse yourself into misery. Mind activities like this will not only change your life but will also change your world views. Remember, you're what you're, don't let anyone change YOUR mind!

8 Tips to Increase Mindfulness

Have you ever had such a stuffy nose that you can't even taste your food? You pass the moves to chew, swallow and digest, but with no gratification or pleasure. Well, this is precisely how many of us encounter our lifetime autopilot that struggles to process the riches and abundance of every moment. The outcome? A life that feels joyful and diluted. But the good news here is if we practice more focus, we will return the magic of daily life. See these eight tips to make the most of your moments.

1. Concentrate on one thing at a time.

Multi-tasking has become a symbol of honor in our constantly hectic lives. By juggling a million tasks to help the children do their homework at once as dinner is going on and testing our handsets, we try to improve our productivity. Multiple tasks are often required, but they simply fragment our concentration, increase tension and reduce the pleasure of any task. Try to start a mission as far as possible and commit to it wholeheartedly. Experience every element and see it done before you start another one. This also refers to eating. Often we expect the next bite before we finish the first! Try to shine a concentrated consciousness light in every moment. You're going to achieve a lot (no stressful loose ends!) and feel a lot less blurred at the end of the day.

2. Breathe.

Our breath is our very strength in life. Focusing on our breath is one of the best ways to reconnect with our bodies nowadays. When you inhale, you can feel the air that reaches your nose and extends your belly, border and lungs. Note how the body flares and opens up as you breathe in. Watch the oxygen slowly leave your body as you exhale, until your belly contracts. What other emotions do you experience when you are breathing? Just be careful. Wherever you are on the bus, you can root at the moment by finding the breath and chasing it like an overflowing wave.

3. Lookout for boring tasks.

We're faced with the boring, everyday things such as standing in line, collecting trash, driving and brushing your teeth. These moments are a nice part of our day, so we can enjoy them! They have far more joy, and texture than the eye meets, provided we pay attention. For example, while standing in line at the grocery store, focus on feeling your two legs firmly planted on the ground. Then look around and take it all in the perfume of the woman before you, the auburn curls on the head of her daughter. Watch the heap of bright apples in the processing area and the colorful line of chocolate bars next to you. Stop thinking of this moment as a means for a purpose, but as a satisfying experience in a living poem of your own right.

4. Control the mind. Watch the mind.

The mind is continually talking about nonsense, usually: what did Susan say yesterday by that comment? Or, I can't believe that I've put five pounds on it! We can often feel overwhelmed by the mind's constantly intrusive thoughts, which take us away from the present moment. But it is useful to note that we are not our thinking – the essential part of our being will stand back and watch the unpredictable machinations of our minds without identifying with them. Any time you overwhelm your thoughts, just remember: "I am not my mind." From the little space or distance, you make, you can root yourself back at the moment, follow your breath, and pay attention to what's going on right then. Suddenly your thoughts will have less control over you and will encourage you to be free.

5. Take the time for what it is.

Many of us slip into the pit of believing that harmony and gladness are the product of our external climate. Regrettably, whatever we are trying to do, difficult or disgusting situations that contradict our preferences are an inevitable part of our lives. So one thing we can alter is how we interpret the moment in which we are. If we can face it precisely, embrace it, warts and all, then we become the protectors of our own inner peace. Facing the facts of life head-on, without avoidance, diversion or misconception, we will gracefully and attentively agree to what it is every moment. Imagine if we were all able to reach an underlying peace source even if it rains on our special day or a long-awaited flight is delayed. What a powerful idea!

6. Meditate.

Meditation may seem uninitiated daunting. However, try not to see it as an effort to silence any thinking that sounds more like an inner war than a calm and grounded experience! When thoughts come and go, just watch them, not get caught in all of the emotions and chaos that they can create. Then let them flutter away and return to your breath again and again. Regular meditation, even if it is only 5 minutes a day, helps you learn more quickly about your everyday exercises and generally leaves you feeling peaceful and quiet.

7. Get innovative.

It is nice to be in the field, inflow, to enjoy the little sweet spot that is what your heart sings. Whether it's cooking, writing, painting or gardening, strive to include as much as possible your favorite things in your life. Sometimes, they are taking your back seat in our busy lives, but if you tap into your sweet spot, you will feel rejuvenated straight away at the heart of mind-complete absorption.

8. Be a boy.

Nothing takes us into the moment except to do something for someone else. We have a warm, glowing sense in the body when we pay compliments, give a meal to a stressed-out neighbor, or write a thank you note. And just listening is one of the kindest gestures we can offer. When you speak to others, instead of concentrating on your next sentence or how you come off, try to give your whole being over to the story of the other person. It is a gift like no other-your consideration, your attentiveness, the gift of attachment.

Know, the focus is a practice. Don't be frustrated if you can't keep it long. Continue to check with you at random times and ask yourself, "Am I being present, or am I lost in the story of my thoughts?" Eventually, with time, you may feel more natural and notice more peace, thanks and joy in your life.

Health Benefits of Tea Flowers and Mindfulness Exercises

The use of Eastern and Early Western medicine flowers and herbs:

Eastern medicine and even early Western medicine have taken advantage of the different benefits of herbs and flowers. Many of these advantages today come in blooming tea, tea made from balls of tea or flowers of tea.

What's a Flower Tea?

A tea flower is identical to a tea ball, hand-sewn leaves of a colorful flower which blooms, normally green or white tea, when dropped in hot water. So the name of the tea is blooming. Flowers and tea are both excellent and delicious.

What kind of floral tea do you have?

A variety of these tea balls are made from different tea leaves and have different flowers, each of which has a distinct and lovely effect. The flowering flowers in tea balls increase the advantages of drinking tea while offering therapeutic fragrance. Each flora has its own unique benefits, including many antioxidant qualities.

Herbal against "True" tea:

Both forms of "true" tea come from the same plant - Camellia sinensis - as against herbal tea. Herbal teas are made from different herbs that are not from the same plant as real tea but can be made like a tea. The key difference between black tea, green tea and oolong tea is how the leaves are handled when selected.

White and Green Tea:

Polyphenols are found in both Green and White Tea. Phenols (a chemical compound that includes an aromatic benzene ring that is bound to the hydroxyl group) are strong antioxidants that bind to free radicals in your body to avoid free radical negative effects.

White tea tends to have more polyphenols and is known to be an antioxidant to combat cancer. Studies at Pace University have shown that white tea extract can delay the growth of staphylococcal infections, pneumonia and dental cavities in bacteria. Researchers claim that white tea will kill species that cause disease.

White tea compounds have also been shown to improve the immune functions of skin cells and to protect the skin from adverse sunlight effects.

Green tea gives people who drink it daily several health benefits. In addition to providing antioxidant benefits, green tea is considered by many as an excellent supplement for weight loss.

Blooming Tea Flowers:

In tea flowers, there are a variety of flowers and flower combinations. Their flavors and aromas vary and enhance your experience by color and elegance.

The benefits include antioxidants that reduce the levels of harmful free radicals, as with green and white tea, that in turn prevent aging and help in a variety of other health fields. Flowers are free of caffeine, while white and green tea contain caffeine.

Osmanthus, jasmine, lily, rose, chrysanthemum, globe amaranth, magnolia, peony, carnation and others are among the styles of flowers used in blooming tea. To read more about and where to find the health benefits of tea flowers, visit A Tea Flower Moment.

Carefulness and tea:

Stress is becoming a significant factor in our worsening health in today's busy, hectic world where we face a devastated economy and violence every day, whether in the media, on the street or in our homes. Stress reductions are significant because of the adverse effects they have on our bodies.

Stress induces improper adrenaline discharge that in turn causes the heart to pump faster and harder, transfers blood at the expense of other organs and muscles, and changes hormones - in particular cortisol, which is an essential hormone for the metabolism of the fat, sugar and protein. A simple habit began in England hundreds of years ago and in Asia thousands of years ago, together with taking advantage of the moment in conscientiousness, will combat the effects of stress.

CHAPTER FOUR
Mindfulness and Meditation

Let's examine in detail how awareness, meditation and awareness can help you live in the moment, relax and release stress and anxiety.

First, ask yourself: is time gone without you being noticed? Look back after days, weeks, months, and even months and ask yourself what happened? Some of us have years without even knowing what has happened. You're wondering, how did I get here? You're not alone if that's you. Most of us have great difficulty nowadays, in the present.

You have ever had a driving experience in your car, and you're at your destination suddenly. It was like you were on the pilot. Your mind thought of other things, something that happened to you already or something in the near or distant future. Where were you driving, exactly? You certainly haven't been there, that's sure!

Living today can be a challenge. You have proven this to yourself already. Right now, I'd like you to do something. Concentrate on the words when you read this paragraph. Really focus. Really focus. Learn how to read one word at a time. Pay attention to the letters, the space between the words, the phrases, the meaning of what you read.

How was that for you? What did you feel? Was it uncomfortable for you? Were you distracted, or were you at that time?

This is another exercise. This is another. You may giggle but go along with it. It could give you a whole new way of being right now.

As your day passes, ask yourself, "Where is my rump?" Sitting on a chair? Do you lean on a desk? Walking down the aisle in the food shop? As stupid as it appears, it's difficult not to be where your bottom is. Being aware and learning to focus and focus does not have to be serious. It's great to lighten up and sometimes more than once. And it's worth it if you do this goofy experiment to make you realize what it is like living in the moment.

Okay. Now that you've tried to rump let's calm down and experience meditation. Meditation is a straightforward and easy exercise to keep you up-to-date and focused. There are so many uses for conscientiousness workouts to alleviate stress and anxiety, tap into your higher consciousness, gain insight into your creativity and imagination, concentrate on a project that is complete, stops procrastination, and calms feelings that wrap you like a warm blanket. These are just a few things that meditation and awareness can help.

It all begins with the most basic functions of life. The breath. The breath. Just like the rump consciousness exercise, let's concentrate on breathing. Stand or sit, don't matter. Stand or sit. Just get conscious of your breath. Throw yourself into a deep breath. Feel the air as the nose enters. Could it be cool? Warm? Warm? Notice that the air passes through your mouth, throat, esophagus and the lungs. Feel a fresh breath in the lungs. Allow the expansion of your lungs. Hold. Hold. Now exhale slowly, pushing the breath out. Do it again. Do it again. Take another profound breath. You will be surprised how quickly you focus and focus on the moment.

If you are anxious, stressed, dispersed, overwhelmed, or have to return to the center, then take a minute to meditate. It's unbelievable what a little attention can do for you. It's your time. Do not let it slip away. Taste it, enjoy it.

MINDFULNESS MEDITATION

Meditation of consciousness is frequently confused with other types of meditation. The main goal of focusing on a specific part of the body or minute is to try and meet a target and develop a skill.

Both modes of concentration are practices such as "Thai-chi" and "Yoga" However, the meditation is different, its aim is to free the mindfully of thoughts, to relax the body so that any thought disappears. This state will last from a few seconds to hours, depending on your capacity. To reach the height of spirituality, you have to reach the height of pure mind.

To accomplish this, you must focus on "sound within yourself" to enter "light within yourself" A distant location at the end of a long dark place. The light is getting closer and closer, and the blessing we receive cannot be clarified when we enter the end of the tunnel and pick up the light. In order to do this, we must enter a pure state through the meditation of mindfulness, "pure" purpose and focus on the "sound" of your inner being.

Meditation on thoughtfulness appears to give us the means to attain mental purity, and there are different methods to be used for successful meditation; all of them use the Refrain, a series of words and sounds that are repeated mentally to help us accomplish our aim. Mantra is sacred, there are many ways of applying Mantra, and no mantra is better than the other, and this state of pure mind is of great importance.

1– Mantra is a very basic, though, and as we repeat in our minds, it becomes more regular and familiar. This thinking is used to replace all our other thoughts, and we substitute the Mantra every time a new thought reaches our mind.

2- In the conscious meditation using the Mantra, we prefer to equate the Mantra with a state of tranquility. The relation is known as Neuro-Linguistic Programming. After preparing for this, when we are tense about something, thinking about the Mantra will take us directly to a state of calm. This makes the Mantra an indispensable weapon for us to cope with the most difficult situations in our lives.

As we understand and how the Mantra works, it becomes apparent that it is not always good to adjust the methods with which the Mantra is applied. Changing Mantra is useful only in specific circumstances where we have to get rid of a habit that keeps us from achieving a particular mental state that does not quite make us. The Motto we use should be reserved for ourselves too, and when we share this knowledge, we give others the ability to manipulate our mind. The best attentive teachers would refrain from offering the best available mantras and focus only on one.

Mantra typically consists of a vowel alternating with some nasal sounds and may include some words. The most common Mantra is "ooooohm or aaaummm", but if we extend our vowel and nasal sound, every other word can do the same. It is best if the Mantra includes a sacred word that means a gift to a Deity, not a generic word with no spiritual world affinity. If you don't want to sing religious chants, you can also use other odd terms to get the same result. Mantra literally means Manas = mind, and Trya = Free Both together make your mind free.

The posture assumed during the meditation is exceptionally significant, with your spine straight and too much relaxation, you will be relaxed and possibly sleeping. Join your hands and spread your legs to match a field of organic energy surrounding you. The traditional Yoga position is another good one, but it requires a particular ability or the position of the fetus.

If you have never attempted meditation for consciousness, find a position and try the following technique:

1- Presume that one of the positions above must be comfortable to meditate effectively.

2- Close your eyes and relax all the muscles, including your face, in your body. Alternatively, breathe and exhale from just one nose. Close your nose with your finger each time you change your breaths.

3- Try to ignore any thought that reaches your mind and try to keep your head clear. If there's a thought, try using a mental mantra-like " oooohhhmmmm " to erase it. You can continue to count and delete thoughts without contemplating them; in five minutes, if you are up to 2 or 3 thoughts, you can meditate effectively.

With a little practice, you should be able to attain independence of thinking in all areas, even though full of people use the Mantra technique. Using the Mantra daily before you have ample meditation practice as a free mind is connected to the thought of the Mantra.

One of the advantages of meditation is that it opens your mind to new thoughts, generates your problems or resolves them. If you put more water out of it, try to think of your mind as a glass full of water. Many smart people meditate daily, Albert Einstein and Edison meditate well through the years in various ways.

Meditation is also described as "listening to silence within the thoughts" this capability is a necessary condition in which you receive "Telepathic Transmissions" you will never be able to hear everyone else's thoughts without silence in your own ideas.

People who regularly practice meditation can be seen very clearly by the way they look and act, which is 10 to 154 years younger than they really are. By breaking away from the thoughts inside our minds daily and allowing our mind's auto-regeneration can bring results beyond our understanding.

Mind Exercises Within Your Yoga Practice

Yoga will offer peace of mind. We generally forget about our burning desire or critical issues. Peace penetrates the mind as well as the body. Here are some yoga exercises that enable you to become relaxed.

1. Start centering

What does center mean? It is a way to turn the mind inward and calm our busy mind. In Kundalini yoga as taught by Yogi Bhajan, at the start of every class and personal practice, a certain mantra is sung. The 'Om' mantra is sung in some hatha yoga lessons. It takes just a few minutes and has a hugely positive effect on our awareness, preparing us for the yoga practice.

The mantra uses a direct influence on the mind, and a chant draws a subtle beginning line which adds something unique to your experience. How would you describe that journey inward - sacred, soulful, or anything else? I too, am fascinated by the different ways in which we describe our experience.

2. Chanting when Practice

We can decide to chant 'Om' aloud in our personal practice at the beginning of the asana portion of our practice. If you begin with a salutation from the sun or moon, you can either sing as you shift in the pose or slow down by chanting an 'Am' while keeping the pose. You may want to explore to find out when chanting is most expected. Do you raise or decrease the intensity of singing while you practice? Does it feel normal after a while to stop singing aloud?

3. Hand Mudra

A traditional hand mudra keeps hands in a place of prayer. This mudra, called the Namaste mudra, can be kept in Tadasana when it is at rest. You should keep your hands on the chest and let your thumbs touch the breast. Notice how every finger rests on its pair and whether one hand hits the other more. Can you equitably divide the burden between the two hands? Do you use excessive effort?

Feel the earth's feet, the hearts' hands, and head to the sky. Next, feel your entire body as one unit, then bring your breath into your consciousness. This rest between poses can become a routine in your personal practice; a pull-in exercise.

You can design your personal practice as a beginner yoga student to include the most useful elements that can calm the mind. When you experiment with these techniques, you may repeatedly discover the power to design your own practice and the ability to calm down your mind.

How to Meditate and Overcoming Mind Chatter

Meditation is an allusive term when you first try this method. Westerners are usually proud of their skills and professional ethics. Meditation is often approached in a way that needs to do something when it could really be defined more appropriately as a method of undoing.

If a new Westerner tries meditation, a frame of mind can be done.

Meditation can be approached more realistically as a way to reach a new direction of failure. Each person's mind is so busy and enigmatic to the extreme. Combining the inherently chaotic mind with the western culture of action will lead to people who have not explored the depths of the environment of which they belong.

The best way to meditate for beginners is to unfold, allow or settle. The beginner doesn't have to do anything. The beginner who wants to begin meditation will first decide if the time is set aside. Time needs to be spent, but don't think about filling the time. Only give yourself time. Meditation, particularly at the beginning, is not so good at running.

If the disposition of the novice is mollified with esthetics, maybe he can light a candle into which one can display the incense, it is perhaps a little bell to signify the start and end of the meditation session. Comfort is helpful, and if a special outfit or clothing is cool, go for it.

There is no need for a hair shirt. Twenty minutes is typically an appropriate time to sit at the outset. When you start to meditation, you will get bored. This is the wild and untamed mind that suggests that we should be up to something more. There are other activities waiting for you. People have to see it.

If you note this, you will know precisely what it means to sit in meditation. You will better deal with the tumultuous mind by taking it back to the object of attention patiently and gently. It's the breath most often, and it could be the flame you have chosen to focus on. You may use a sign like a chickadee.

The most well-known technique is to look at the breath, but this is your meditation. The only outcome you need is to relax your mind. Meditation is a process, and you just have to invest in time and patience to realize the benefits.

It's not difficult to learn how to meditate for beginners. You actually do it every day without even noticing it.

"mind chatter" is one of the most daunting challenges to tackle. It is essential to realize beforehand that mental talk is natural when you start any form of meditation routine. Many people avoid chatting about their minds, become depressed, stop saying, "Meditation doesn't work."

A strong thumb rule: resistance = stamina. You avoid the chat and try to ignore it so that the chatter of mind becomes louder and more distracting. You offer energy and strength to these negative thoughts.

It's time to change the strategy of your game! Start by recognizing and observing the chat. You will note the thoughts that start to run through your mind will trigger feelings of anger and anxiety. It's not shocking that people stop meditating. Who needs that to feel!

The great news is that this is the best things about meditation and empowerment in your scope, being a master of your own thinking!

Try it, the next time you sit down to meditate, start by looking at yourself as a giant looking down into a giant boxing ring. All your thoughts begin to reach the ring and begin to knock. Don't enter the ring; just look at the thoughts to the ring. Some proposals can be more harmful than others, but it doesn't matter because you aren't in the ring.

When the thoughts start to tire and vanish, the match is over. Now we shift to our own silence and silence. Just try to breathe, continue to breathe and fill your lungs with fresh oxygen.

I know the scenario sounds corny, but it works absolutely. Essentially you monitor your own thoughts and say hey, I will give you about 2 minutes to complain and then I will move on. You would be surprised at how the life of the mind evaporates. And you did not once lose control and let your thinking be carried out.

Meditation - The Key to Success

Meditation is a unique and fundamental way of healing the mind naturally. Meditation is now the most sought-after cure for all. Yet it is also ignored and misinterpreted by many self-styled gurus. And do not be fooled by any of these gourmets' advertisements and preaching. Instead, please do some research alone and figure them out honestly. Check your suitability before you join any group of persons or organization.

Every individual is blessed with a unique mind, great inner power and energy that unlocks more when he starts meditating. It will naturally lead him on the journey. So start meditating without much hesitation or waiting for a guru of a sect as soon as possible. There is basically no need for somebody's support. It's effortless and easy to do.

How to ponder:

Ideal, with your eyes closed for several minutes every day, preferably after a bath, swimming or a workout or thinking about something. The body and mind are new and after a good bath in a natural rhythm. You may either sit on the chair, stand or cross the legs on the floor. Note, your backbone must be straight always in any place you meditate.

The whole body must not be strained but relaxed with the right stance. In the early days of meditation, introspection takes place on its own. It's a phenomenon of nature. Meditation is more effective if done in silence without noise or events in the community. While other meditation techniques exist, this is the most successful and time-consuming approach, and the results are much more efficient and lifelong.

Introspection and meditation are interconnected. Introspection means the study on the subconscious level of one's own ideas and behaviors of one's mind. When daily meditation is performed, introspection takes place only for the first few minutes. It automatically saves useful items and deletes discarded information.

This is our mind's magic.

When the mind is free of its ideas and fears, it paves the way for a smooth and straightforward journey into the unknown. Deep meditation starts here alone. It's a phenomenon of nature. Only sit preferably without walking and doing something. Only continue to flow and float away with the flow. Relax and enjoy this newly discovered bliss every moment. That's the only way to get there. It cannot be explicitly initiated without the disturbance, emotions, ideas, fears or conflicts of the mind.

Meditation is a way to steer the mind to the unconscious level to slow down its mental work processes gradually. This helps us to take some time to rest and relax. If we can meditate every day, we can unload significant items daily from our minds. Although the actual period of relaxation can vary from a few seconds to just a few minutes, it still makes a considerable difference. It helps to relieve many thoughts and fears that block the psychic energies to enable the mind to operate more smoothly and effectively. If you begin to practice meditation on a regular basis, you will soon feel the positive changes in your life. It could be about your clarity to think, study and learn new things. It also helps to remember and remember details, evaluate and resolve issues, emotional intelligence and relationships, etc.

There is another meditation form that is often recommended to people. You should meditate in this way with your eyes wide open. All those who cannot meditate with their eyes closed are advised that this approach starts to meditate with open eyes. Here, people are centered on a single object. It could be a flickering candle or a black dot on the wall. Both should be held at 2-3 meters' distance, which is clearly visible to the eyes. No movement or noise of any sort should take place so that an appropriate concentration can be established. It's easy with a little practice.

The key concept here is to avoid participating in all other tasks, to sit still in a certain place and concentrate on an object. This approach seems successful, but the mind still works here. Secondly, there was no decluttering of the mind. It seems to be working at first. But people gradually start to lose confidence because even after several days it doesn't produce good results. That's pretty normal. Whenever you begin to notice good results, your mind will be more inclined and inspired to proceed.

The meditation process is completed through four steps:

First of all, the link between the mind and everyday life and events should be cut for a few minutes.

Secondly, it's about declutching and riding the mind of the discarded stuff which further unlocks the mental energies.

Third, the mind should relax, and the revived mental energy should be guided at better efforts.

Fourth, all seven chakras, centers of the energy of the body, are to be gradually washed, triggered and energized.

The rhythm of the body and mind thus continues to function incompleteness and synchronization. It helps to address the different mental and physical conditions that have evolved over the years.

Neurological conditions are the most helpful, the effects of which can be seen only after a few days.

Since meditation is not a religious practice or ritual, no laws or regulations exist. But there are some necessary precautions to make your thoughts and experiences feel more optimistic.

The following are:

Consult the doctor when you have any physical disorder often, if you start to experience any pressure when sitting or standing in a position for a longer time, but note that during meditation, the backbone must be straight.

Interact with a handful of people who meditate for a while. You will learn about the advantages, perspectives and other avenues you might create.

A comfortable place for meditation should be used: No dumb smell, shouldn't be too hot, too cold, unendurable moisture or humidity, shouldn't be too brightly lit and damp dark etc. In short, space appropriate and relaxing for you can be selected for meditation. Or even a spot in a forest, a lake, a river or a waterfall, but without noise or other distractions.

Stop Mediation During pain: Adequate rest or when disease happens, other discomfort or when the mind and body are exhausted. A break in these conditions is a long-term gain.

CHAPTER FIVE

Running Techniques - New Ways to Add Fun to Your Run

There are between 30 and 40 million runners in the U.S., according to Running USA, 8 and 16 million are known as regular runners (defined as those who run a minimum of 100 days during the year). These statistics show clearly how popular a hobby sport is in America.

However, these statistics suggest problems too, that is to say, in spite of a large number of regular runners in America, about 10-20 million runners are occasional or intermittent. It is also a reasonable belief that many people are lax in their running routines mainly because of their fornication (as cited by a number of studies that have demonstrated a strong correlation between boredom and levels of exercise).

But boredom must not lessen the satisfaction or frequency of your selected sport. Indeed, advanced running methods make fun of their runs and reduce the chances of boredom. Cross-training, periodization and technical inspiration are three of the most common strategies.

Training Cross

Crossing or temporary exercising is one of the most common methods for a simple purpose - battling the boredom and preparing the body in a new (more productive) way. Many cross-training routes a runner may use to fight forbearance while still training the body enough for the next race.

In the sea. In the water. Swimming pool exercises, especially "water running," have proven to be a useful training medium for runners. The flooding of water avoids the effect on the muscles and joints that are so normal during paving while still offering intense, complete body workouts.

At the gym. Running around a track or a workstation is not the only equipment based in the gym that can enhance running techniques. In reality, standard exercise equipment including stationary bicycles, elliptical machinery, and stair climbers imitate running movements and add a variety to running.

In the studio workout. While not always listed in the same category as running, studio exercises such as yoga and Pilates have proven useful to runner cross-training. These two types of exercise stretch and stretch the muscles, in particular the leg muscles, which are essential for runners.

Periodization

This refers to the technique that top race athletes use to maximize their training advantages while preventing boredom. They divided their training year into one or two months. They change their training schedule slightly for each new section of the year. This typically involves just modifying one exercise a week, slightly different from the rest of the week's training routine.

There are several ways to incorporate this practice. For e.g., if you usually run a route, turn once a week over one of the cycles to run on another surface/setting (like an outdoor trail). If you usually work at a steady but moderate speed, turn to interval training (where for many minutes you run at the maximum limit of your ability for a pre-defined number of sets) once a week. If you usually run alone, turn once a week to work with a friend (or a group).

Periodization cannot only reverse boredom but also avoid a certain training regimen from making the body too relaxed. Studies have shown that the body becomes increasingly effective in daily exercise activities over time, such that the same routines are no longer of the same health benefits. The addition of a new routine to the mix will reinvigorate the mind and body.

Motivation for technology

Boredom is a motor zapper Fortunately; many technical motivations have shown that boredom is lowered and running techniques improved.

Music. Runners take to the road or path with increased excitement with the advent of the Walkman and (now) the iPod. Many studies have shown that the effort, as well as the boredom of a repetitive activity like running, can interrupt the music. Research into the use of music in exercise has shown that participants frequently experience a decreased sense of effort (measured as an RPE) while exercising with music at a particular level of exercise intensity. Music, it seems, distracts the mind of the runner and positions him in a better setting.

Trackers for speed and distance. While runners used such devices as "step and mile counters" to track their running devices' speed and distance with often dubious precision for a long time, the Nike + Sports Kit has brought them into a whole new dimension. By using GPS technology, the Sports Kit includes a sensor inserted into a suitable Nike sneaker. This sensor measures the size, speed and calories burned and transmits these data to your iPhone or iPod Touch wirelessly.

Monitors Heart Rate. Many heart rating sensors use the same GPS technology to simply check the heart rate to measure the pace (by insertable shoe pads), which gives a fuller image of changes to training. It also offers a visual interface, via a computer screen "wrist-wearable" to track progress.

E-Motivation. In a not too distant past, people formed communities to support them in their selected sports. Such peer reinforcement has proved to be a good motivator. But today it is no longer appropriate to join the party physically. You can carry the party to you now, instead. Nike + is one of the websites for athletic merchandise providing runners (and other athletes) with a platform to connect with each other and support each other. In addition, many of these websites have features, including progress trackers, customized exercise plans and activity logs, which can minimize frustration, while encouraging them to learn new (and enhanced) running techniques.

Many runners have employed these strategies to avoid boredom effectively and to sustain their routines. Each technique has added to its runs an element of novelty or fun. You may also change these commonly used approaches with a little effort and imagination in order to satisfy your own unique needs in terms of improved operating techniques.

What Makes a Perfect Running Technique?

There is actually a reason why you can't measure your running success accurately. Although running doesn't have many things like other sports, you still need to figure out what variables are so that you can get the maximum out of running. One of the most critical factors to look after if the gear you use is to run correctly. You must select the right socks, shoes, shorts and running ground to ensure maximum benefit. The other factor that stands out from the crowd is the technique they use.

Many experts emphasize, and they have all the right to say, that your technique determines your performance. If you use the right methods, you will improve your muscle performance and lower your chances of being injured. While runners who want to lose weight need different techniques than those who wish to compete in marathons, constant things make up a perfect running technique:

1- Breathing:

Every time teaching peoples to run insist that they need to learn how to breathe properly in order to run correctly. Like any other sport, running requires a high supply of oxygen to keep the muscles performing. The recommendation to you is to inhale as much air as possible with your nose and mouth. Using your diaphragm, you will have more room to store oxygen in place of your chest so that your muscles can get enough of it.

2- Posture running:

I know that when they see it, everybody can recognize the professional position. The location of your head, shoulders and legs will quickly improve your running efficiency. The thing you should remember is that during your running session, you must remain consistent and consistent. If you do not, you may end up injuring yourself. If you lean your body forward, you will use gravity to increase your speed.

3- Scale:

I'm sure you don't want to put all the stress on just one leg. To preserve your equilibrium, and action must be distributed equally on the body's muscles. Leaning forward can help you speed up, but it can also impact your equilibrium if you don't do it properly.

How to Run with Speed and Ease

Were you aware that running is one of the most dangerous injury sports?

Maybe that's because 9 out of 10 runners have never got any technical instructions! I'm not just about casual riders - even those who routinely pound their pavement over long distances or at a mid-elite stage have often been driven little or no direction.

In principle, everyone can run without the manual - just take your legs, pump your arms and do it. Right?

Guess again.

This is definitely the path most people follow and can only work out for you if you are biomechanically ideal, with natural athletic skills and inherent balance, core stability and posture.

If that sounds like you, don't miss the rest of this post.

If, in truth, you're not a robot, read on.

I'll teach you the essential information you need to significantly increase your speed and endurance while beginning the painless running phase.

Have you ever seen a very great runner in action? Maybe on TV, or perhaps in your local park or track. You know the man - the unusual person who seems to run mühelos and with pleasure.

Next time you observe one of these blessed few gliding by, resist driving them up and observing their movements instead. You'll note that their postures are sound, their gestures fluid and their symmetry beautiful to watch. They appear light on their feet. If applied consistently, the following techniques will allow you to work with the same ease and grace as anybody.

Six Plus to Be A Better Runner

1. Breath

Many runners appear to squeeze the air like a fish out of the sea, open their mouths, jut up and breathe. It shouldn't be that difficult! Respiring through the mouth reduces your cardiovascular capacity and increases the body's burden and tension. The ultimate result is close to attempting to swim upstream. Right respiration should be in and out of the nose, except in intense exercise where you breathe out through the mouth when necessary. The breath should start in your belly (diaphragm) and finally, get into your chest. You must first practice at a slow or steady pace. I've seen a lot of runners whose speed, stance and overall technique have greatly improved.

2. Body Awareness

Stand before a mirror, close your eyes. Hold your eyes closed for 2 to 3 minutes and concentrate on your posture and balance. Start your feet - they're meant to be parallel. Then focus on aligning your elbows, knees, hips, and eventually your shoulders. Make sure the arms are slightly bent, loosely hanging. Your head should be absolutely straight 'on.' Open your eyes until you are confident of your place. How close have you been? Note where 'off track' you've gone. Keep these deviations in mind when you launch your next race. You would be surprised if you could really see how you look when you run out of exhaustion. Before every race, practising body knowledge gives you a better understanding of how to hold and correct your body when running. Ideal alignment is one of the main keys to a smooth running without pain.

3. Stop Using Your Legs and Arms

Try to jog for ten seconds on the spot. Immediately after that, walk 10 seconds on the spot. What's faster - what would you use the least energy if you were for 2 hours to do it? Many people suggest that they move – and they will be right. This is because you learned to run by pumping your legs and arms and mostly by twisting your calf muscles to lift your feet off balls. Your calf's muscles are a tiny set - it's no wonder that you're tired of using them to lift your entire body. You use hip flexors as you gather your legs to walk. These are one of your core's largest strongest muscles which link your trunk to your legs. They are supposed to propel you forward. One of the best tricks to run smoothly is to learn from your heart. Your heart consists of your abdominal inner and outer muscles, as well as your hip folding (psoas) and numerous stabilizing lower back muscles. You just need to understand each of these muscles to get full core sensitivity. Draw your belly button into your spinal cord and use your hip flexors to collect your legs when running slowly. Consider your heart as your nucleus, which is the source of all power, strength and stability.

4. Understand Rotation

We just told you we didn't use your legs, but we didn't even use your weapons. This is where rotation enters. Rotation is one of the sport's most essential elements. - when you step forward, your spine rotates. In reality, a study with a legless man showed him walking through the room with his core rotational skills alone. You would never have noticed from the waist that he had no legs. This tells us how strong our rotational muscles can become and also shows the value of rotation in operation. The arms and legs are merely core helpers and rotating ability. With any kind of twisting movement like a wooden cable cut and with dynamic rotational stretching, you can boost your rotation. Try holding a small ball in front of your chest between your two palms. Practice the heart and hips rotating without tensing or shifting your muscles. When running, try adding core rotation rather than pumping your muscles.

5.Relax Your Body - Focus Your Mind

It's all very well to use running as a chance to stop and prepare the day ahead, but your approach doesn't help. A concentrated mind helps you to understand and regulate your heart, alignment and breathing. Be alert not only with your movements but also with your thoughts. How do you respond to some rough terrain? Tense the muscles and think about the tough job ahead. Relax. Run a search for the top of the foot. Remember how patient you have been to run with good technique. Up the hill, change your move and simply 'go with the breeze' accordingly. Relaxation is almost more difficult than any other skill, but excessive muscle stress not only reduces your blood circulation (speed reduction) but also raises your risk of muscle weakness and injury. Maybe it's worth your time to master muscle relaxation and concentrate your mind on using the heart and breathing to move you forward.

6. Win The Race Slow And Steady

At last, don't try overnight to change any aspect of your running. You'll probably get fed up for one thing and want to give it up. On the other side, your body obviously cannot process and use all of this information at once. Small improvements are necessary – why not focus on one of the previous steps every week.

Step by step, you will take advantage of modern strategies to your body and reduce your risk of injury.

Practice Mindfulness for Joy and Peace

Life can be busy with the quick speed of jobs, work, transfers and childcare. You should, however, find time to practice more harmony and joy in your life. People think about the economy, their finances and their future. It can definitely trigger a lot of tension, which can contribute to mood and physical changes in turn.

Research shows that most people would like to slow down more frequently and smell the roses. You're feeling rushed. You live in a fast way trying to achieve your goals and do what you need to, but when you get home at night and complete the tasks at night, you are not tired. Most encounters at one time or another burnout. Most are worried about anxiety and depressive disorders. Some only sound like machines - they have little to no joy.

I have good news for you if you feel anything like what I have just mentioned. Researchers have researched the practice of attention to stress, depression and have found that it actually reduces depressive symptoms and allows people to live happier and healthier lives. Consciousness is overgrowing around the world, as this methodology means that more and more people are witnessing tremendous changes.

What is Mindfulness?

Attention basically means that you are mindful of your current thoughts and body functions. At this moment, it is "mindful" of your feelings. Jon Kabat-Zinn, a research fellow at the Medical School of the University of Massachusetts, has helped make Zen Buddhist meditation popular in recent years. He has done comprehensive research into the impact of focus on stress, emotions and chronic pain and disease. Attention has been shown to decrease depressive symptoms, chronic lessen pain, eating disorder aid and drug misuse and minimize anxiety. It performs so well that some hospitals use it as a method for current therapy.

Sweet Old Days

Remember the days you were a child or a girl? You most probably didn't have a lot of questions or feelings. Kids are better able to think less and play more. They are more concerned about discovering their worlds and only enjoying life now. They don't feel guilty about their history and don't care about the future.

But as kid grow older, they start to live less in the present moment and more in the past and in the future. Their thoughts significantly increase, more pain and negative feelings begin to arise, and life becomes more difficult. They will start wrestling with fear, anxiety or depression, and sometimes struggle against these negative feelings; they can aim to get things done. You could try alcohol, food, jobs, etc. The problem is that these problems are not going away with pain or unpleasant feelings so that they only get profoundly suppressed or stuffed.

By adulthood, several negative thoughts can run roughly through your head, and your humor can represent this. They allowed negative thoughts to prevail. You lost contact with that naive young child who simply liked to live and enjoy the simple things of life in the present moment.

Please note that meditation will help people avoid living in the past and in the future and start living in the moment. It makes you relax and slow down; it smells the flowers and enjoys every moment. When you practice consciousness, negative thoughts and feelings are lost, and a sense of liberation, happiness and joy is felt.

How to practice focus

Practising attention is quite easy. Only find a calm place to sit down, take a couple of deep breaths and relax each inch. Your purpose is to be mindful of your current moment and to forget about the past or the future. Concentrate on your breath as you breathe in and out.

Feel the air entering your lungs when you respire. When you exhale, concentrate on exhaling harmful elements in you.

When you concentrate on breathing, you will NOT rely on other things by default. If random thoughts come, simply notice the thought and turn your attention in and out.

Take time every day to sit and practice awareness meditation. In the early weeks, try 10-15 minutes, but then try 30 minutes a day. This may seem like a long time to sit still but bear in mind that you are battling stress, depression, frustration and all kinds of negative feelings that have invaded your mind for decades while you practice conscience.

Do you know what you're going to find when you practice attention? Your days are going to be happier. Throughout the days, you will be conscious of your breathing. You will enjoy your current moments even more during the day. When you sit on the road for an hour after work, instead of getting frustrated, you're relaxed, calmer and happy just because you are alive and breathing.

You will be more involved in the lives of your spouse and children. You will connect more lovingly with others. You will be more appropriate, less judgmental; more connected, more sympathetic and emotionally secure to your spiritual self.

Go ahead and launch your journey of knowledge today. Engage to slow down and smell the flowers. I hope you're delighted with the outcome. After all, we all want to be caring, peaceful and cheerful, so, if consciousness is a ticket, let's do it!

CONCLUSION

There are about as many reasons to run as the days of the year. If you're still considering if you are to run, check out the reasons why you should and by the end of that list, you're going to be in the store to buy your first real one.

Okay, so this is the first excuse to start running, but it's still a fantastic one. Running can be daunting at first, but you would want to see improvements in your body and your numbers faster. If that is your initial incentive, you can also use it as your motivation to keep tossing a photo in the fridge beforehand. Every day you will see it to remind you to run and if you want food to remind you of nothing!

Let's face it, you probably have a lot of stress throughout your life, whether it's your career, your family or something, but you can actually feel much better if you start running. Studies have shown over and over that you can potentially reduce the tension you are feeling while exercising. Reducing your stress will make your job more effective and help you do more at home, practically making your running more efficient.

While you might not go out and find a running group once you get started, you may find that you want people to ride with after a short time. A running group will let you meet new people, and some people meet their future wife just by going out and running, even though that's not how you can make new lifelong friends and feel better about yourself.

Running is one of the best things to do, all you need to do is a proper running plan or running guide and a good pair of shoes, and you will have a happier life from now on.

Made in United States
Troutdale, OR
05/13/2024

19831341R00051